SPEED SKATING

GLOBAL CITIZENS: OLYMPIC SPORTS

Published in the United States of America by Cherry Lake Publishing
Ann Arbor, Michigan
www.cherrylakepublishing.com

Content Adviser: Liv Williams, Editor, www.iLivExtreme.com
Reading Adviser: Marla Conn MS, Ed., Literacy specialist, Read-Ability, Inc.

Photo Credits: ©Iurii Osadchi / Shutterstock.com, cover, 9, 13, 15, 16, 27; Image from: Jensens / Wikimedia
Commons / Public Domain, 5; ©Milosz Maslanka / Shutterstock.com, 7; ©Paolo Bona / Shutterstock.com, 10,
17, 28; ©Gertan / Shutterstock.com, 14; ©Sander van Ginkel / Wikimedia Commons, 18; ©StockphotoVideo /
Shutterstock.com, 21; ©McSmit / Wikimedia Commons, 22; ©Scharfsinn / Shutterstock.com, 25;

Library of Congress Cataloging-in-Publication Data

Names: Labrecque, Ellen, author.
Title: Speed skating / by Ellen Labrecque.
Description: Ann Arbor, Michigan : Cherry Lake Publishing, 2018. | Series: Global citizens: Olympic sports |
    Includes bibliographical references and index.
Identifiers: LCCN 2017033463 | ISBN 9781534107557 (hardcover) | ISBN 9781534109537 (pdf) |
    ISBN 9781534108547 (pbk.) | ISBN 9781534120525 (hosted ebook)
Subjects: LCSH: Speed skating—Juvenile literature. | Winter Olympics—Juvenile literature.
Classification: LCC GV850.3 .L33 2018 | DDC 796.91/4—dc23
LC record available at https://lccn.loc.gov/2017033463

Cherry Lake Publishing would like to acknowledge the work of The Partnership for 21st Century Learning.
Please visit *www.p21.org* for more information.

Printed in the United States of America
Corporate Graphics

ABOUT THE AUTHOR

Ellen Labrecque has written over 100 books for children. She loves the Olympics and has
attended both the Winter and Summer Games as a reporter for magazines and television.
She lives in Yardley, Pennsylvania, with her husband, Jeff, and her two young "editors,"
Sam and Juliet. When she isn't writing, she is running, hiking, and reading.

TABLE OF CONTENTS

CHAPTER 1

History: Speed Skating

The first Winter Olympics was held in Chamonix, France, from January 25 to February 5, 1924. It included 258 athletes from 16 different countries competing in 16 events. Since then, the Winter Olympics has been held every 4 years in a number of countries. (The Games were skipped in 1940 and 1944 during World War II.) As the Games progressed, more competitors and events were added. Fast-forward to the 2014 Winter Games held in Sochi, Russia. There were 2,873 competitors from 88 different countries competing in 98 events. That's a lot more competitors and events!

From the graceful choreography of figure skating to the lightning-speed action in hockey, the Winter Games display some of the most unbelievable sports and athletes. Speed skating is no exception as it is one of the fastest sports in the Winter Olympics.

The European speed skating championship in 1911.

The Story of Skating

Speed skating has been around for more than 3,000 years. At first, people from Scandinavia (present-day Denmark, Norway, Finland, and Sweden) and the Netherlands made skates with blades from animal bones! They strapped these blades to their boots to skate across frozen rivers and lakes. It was a form of rapid transportation during the long, grueling winters. Researchers believe that people used these early blades to dart away from danger and to hunt for food.

Some sources say that in the late 1500s a Scotsman upgraded the dull bone blades to sharp iron ones, yet others suggest that it was the Dutch. Whether it were the Scots or the Dutch that made the upgrade first, this change led to skating becoming popular as both a **recreational** activity and a competitive sport. In 1642, the first speed skating club was established in Edinburgh, Scotland. The United States didn't officially organize a speed skating club until 1849 in Philadelphia, Pennsylvania— more than 200 years after Scotland!

Speed skating transitioned from a form of transportation to a fun winter activity and finally to a competitive sport in the late 1700s. On February 4, 1793, the first speed skating race took place in England, stretching over 15 miles (24 kilometers). Then, in 1889, the first World Championships were held in the Netherlands. The first short track speed skating championship was held 17 years later, in 1906.

People used to strap the blades onto their boots.

Long Track Speed Skating

Long track speed skating is when skaters race against the clock on a 400-meter (1,312-foot) track. Each race only has two racers in it. The skater with the fastest time after everybody skates is declared the winner. At the 1932 Olympics in Lake Placid, New York, the organizers decided to run the long track races in a mass start as opposed to skating against the clock in pairs. This was a big advantage for the North American skaters who had been practicing like this all along. The United States won four speed skating gold medals that year. Many countries, especially the ones in Europe, were against this change. By the following Olympics in 1936, the sport reverted back to skating in pairs.

Every event is skated in pairs except for the team pursuit, which is skated in teams of three. The mass start event is officially a new event at the 2018 Olympics. Twenty-four skaters will all start at the same time and race for 16 laps.

The women's speed skating event officially made its Olympic debut
at the 1960 Games.

Short track athletes competing at the 2006 Games.

Short Track Speed Skating

Short track speed skating is when skaters race in packs of up to six people on a shorter track. The course, which is 196.8 feet (60 m) long and 98.4 ft (30 m) wide, has four rubber blocks in the corners. The skaters must go around the blocks when they skate. Short track is a lot like roller-skating races on oval tracks.

Short track was born out of the lack of long track speed skating courses. Because North America did not have many 400-meter (1,312 ft) ice rinks, skaters practiced on smaller ice hockey rinks. However, this meant skaters had to develop different skills, such as learning how to take tighter turns and skating on shorter **straightaways**. North American rules were soon developed for these shorter courses.

The International Skating Union (ISU) declared short track an official sport in 1967. Twenty-five years later, it was added to the Winter Olympic program at the 1992 Games in Albertville, France. Four events were held that year: men's 1,000-meter (3,281 ft), men's 5,000-meter (16,404 ft) relay, women's 500-meter (1,640.4 ft), and women's 3,000-meter (9,842.5 ft) relay.

Developing Claims and Using Evidence

The blades on skates have become stronger and sharper as new technology has been invented. Short track speed skaters skate very close together, yet try to pass each other to gain an advantage. Athletes have been severely injured in crashes when competitors' blades slice into them. As a result, some people think the sport has gotten too dangerous. Other fans say the riskier and more exciting, the better short track is to watch. Using evidence you found, form your own opinion. Do you think short track speed skating at the Olympics has become too dangerous? Why or why not?

CHAPTER 2

Geography: The Netherlands and South Korea Rule!

At the 2014 Winter Olympics, 179 athletes from 23 nations participated in at least one of the long track speed skating events, and 116 athletes from 25 nations participated in one of the short track events. But when it came to winning a medal in long track speed skating, one country stood far from the rest: the Netherlands! At the 2014 Sochi Games, the Netherlands won 23 of the 30 medals awarded in long track speed skating. This is the most dominant performance by one country in a single sport at a Winter Olympics to date. The country has also won

As of the 2014 Games, Ireen Wüst of the Netherlands has won eight Olympic medals, half of which are gold.

105 Olympic speed skating medals total. Norway is the second best at long track speed skating, but has only won 80 medals total. Unfortunately, it did not win any at the 2014 Games.

Netherlands' Advantage

Why is the Netherlands so good at this sport? One simple answer is because of its canal system. The Netherlands is a country filled with canals. Amsterdam, the capital city, has 31 miles (50 km) of canals alone. When they freeze, people

The Netherlands also hold many speed skating competitions for its citizens.

use them to skate all over the place. This canal system may have led to the Netherlands' advantage in long track speed skating. The Netherlands also has eight professional speed skating clubs and more than 20 long track ice rinks. The whole country is only about twice the size of New Jersey. In contrast, the entire United States has just six long track ice rinks and no professional clubs.

Maria Lamb of the United States competes at the 2014 Games.

Jorien ter Mors (right) of the Netherlands won two gold medals at the 2014 Games.

If one athlete falls during a speed skating event, it can affect others, too.

Sportswoman of the World!

The most dominant long track speed skater from the most dominant country (the Netherlands) is Ireen Wüst. She has won eight Olympic medals (four of them gold) over the past three Olympics (2006, 2010, 2014). At the 2014 Games, she won two gold and three silver. This was the most medals for any one athlete at the entire Games.

At the 2014 Games, Silovs races to catch up to Mark Tuitert of the Netherlands.

South Korea Rules Short Track Speed Skating

South Korea has won more short track speed skating medals (42 medals total), including more gold (21), than any other country. China comes in second, with 30 medals total, nine of which are gold. Why is South Korea so good at short track? It may be because kids learn the sport starting as early as elementary school! If the kids are skilled enough, they may even start training with the country's national team.

[21ST CENTURY SKILLS LIBRARY]

Going Long *and* Short

Haralds Silovs of Latvia is the only athlete in history to compete in both long track (16,404 ft or 5,000 m) and short track (4,921 ft or 1,500 m) events in the Olympics. At the 2010 Games in Vancouver, Canada, Silovs finished in 20th place in his long track event and 10th place in his short track event. He did this not only at the same Olympics but on the same day! Although he was disappointed in his finishing places, he did say competing in both races on the same day was just a "little crazy."

Gathering and Evaluating Sources

As of the 2018 Games, there have been 23 Winter Olympics held in 20 cities. Using the Internet and your local library, list the host cities by country. What countries have hosted the Winter Games the most? What countries have hosted the least? Why do you think some countries host the Winter Olympics more times than others?

CHAPTER 3

Civics: Olympic Pride

Participating in the Olympics can be a big source of pride for countries. Fans come and wave their country's flag and cheer for their favorite athletes. They may even display their country's colors in unusual ways.

The Netherlands loves to cheer on its long track speed skating team. Nicknamed the Orange Clad Crazies at the 2014 Olympics, the Netherlands fans wore giant orange wigs and painted their faces orange to match their country's sport color. The Netherlands has so much Olympic pride that even its royal family, whose dynasty name is House of Orange-Nassau, flew all the way to Sochi, Russia, to cheer on their team at the 2014 Games.

Dutch fans go all out to support their favorite athletes.

Winning Medals Equals Higher Television Ratings

People want to watch winners! When a country's athlete is competing to win a medal at the Olympics, its television ratings usually soar. In South Korea, 10.9 million people watched their speed skater Lee Sang-Hwa win gold in the 500-meter (1,640.4 ft) race at the 2014 Games. This was one of the largest audiences ever for an Olympic event in that country.

Kramer has a total of seven Olympic medals.

More than 4.5 million viewers in the Netherlands (nearly 30 percent of the population) watched as Sven Kramer won a gold medal in the 2014 men's 5,000-meter (16,404 ft) speed skating final. This was the largest television audience for anything in the Netherlands since the previous year.

People in China love to watch short track speed skating. The sport's events delivered the 2014 Game's top three ratings in China. The biggest audience, 21 million people, was for the men's 1,000-meter (3,281 ft) event.

The Ambassadors

Olympic cities ask athletes to be **ambassadors** for their Games. The athletes promote the Olympics to fans around the world. One of the ambassadors of the 2018 Games is speed skater Lee Sang-Hwa of South Korea. She won the gold medal in the 500-meter (1,640.4 ft) event at the 2010 and 2014 Olympics and hopes to do it again in 2018. She is one of the most famous athletes in all of South Korea. And since her country is hosting the Games in 2018, her races will draw even bigger crowds!

Developing Claims

In 2011, South Korean short track speed skater Ahn Hyun-Soo became a Russian citizen. So instead of competing for South Korea at the 2014 Games, he changed his name to Viktor Ahn and skated for Russia. He won three gold medals for his new country. Why do you think he switched countries? Should Olympic athletes have to compete for the country in which they were born? Why or why not?

CHAPTER 4

Economics: Speed Skating Is Big Business

Hosting the Olympic Games costs a lot of money. Reports revealed that the 2018 Winter Olympics in PyeongChang, South Korea, could cost more than $10 billion! The city hopes to earn back a lot of that money once the Olympics begins.

The Fans

Tourists come to the city to see the Olympics. They spend money by staying in hotels, buying souvenirs, and eating in the city's restaurants. Speed skating, one of the Winter Olympics'

The Gangneung Ice Arena will hold the short track events at the 2018 Games.

biggest events, is especially big in South Korea. The country hopes to draw as many as 20,000 tourists and fans to the Gangneung Oval (the long track **venue**) and the Gangneung Ice Arena (the short track venue). The country expects both venues to sell out during the competitions. The more tourists and fans that come and watch speed skating, the more money they spend and give back to the host city.

The Sponsors

Advertisers like Coca-Cola and McDonald's pay a lot of money to sponsor the Olympics. Their signs and logos appear in television commercials and on boards all over the venues. Clothing companies supply the uniforms and the outfits for the opening and closing ceremonies. Under Armour made the US speed skating uniforms for the 2014 Games and will continue to do so in 2018 and 2022. However, in 2014, the US team failed to win a medal in speed skating, and many skaters blamed their Under Armour suits for slowing them down. They even switched mid-Olympics to old Under Armour uniforms to see if it would improve their time. It didn't. The **chief executive officer** (CEO) of Under Armour, Kevin Plank, promised that their suits will be better than ever in time for the 2018 Games.

Speed Skaters Give Big Bucks

In the United States, it isn't easy for speed skaters to make a lot of money. They don't appear in a lot of commercials or get paid a lot by sponsors. Short track speed skater Apolo Anton Ohno, now retired, was one exception. He was sponsored by big

US speed skaters blamed Under Armour for their less than stellar performance at the 2014 Games.

Ohno retired from speed skating in 2013.

Taking Informed Action

Do you want to learn more about the Winter Olympics and speed skating? There are many different organizations that you can explore. Check them out online. Here are three to start your search:

- Olympic—Speed Skating: Learn more about the history of long track speed skating at the Olympics.
- Team USA—Speed Skating: Learn about short track and long track in the United States on the US team's official website.
- NBC Olympics: Find out all you can about the 2018 Winter Olympic Games in PyeongChang, South Korea.

companies like Subway and Coca-Cola and was the highest paid short track speed skater in US history to date. He made more than $10 million in his career, thanks to his gold medal skating. Ohno won eight medals total (including two gold) over the course of three Winter Olympic seasons (2002, 2006, and 2010).

Ohno uses his money and fame to help other people. He is involved in many charities that help sick and poor people all over the world. He has even started his own foundation to promote healthy habits in young people. "It has really inspired me to be a better person," Ohno says about his involvement in different charities.

Communicating Conclusions

Before reading this book, did you know a lot about speed skating and the Winter Olympics? Now that you know more, why do you think both long track and short track aren't as popular in the United States as they are in other countries? Would establishing college speed skating teams and professional leagues help? Why or why not?

Think About It

When people think of risky Olympic sports, speed skating may come to mind. It's no wonder—these athletes can reach speeds of over 32 miles (52 kilometers) per hour for men and over 30 mph (49 kph) for women! In short track speed skating during the 2010 Games, 28 percent of men suffered injuries, but only 9 percent of women did. Why do you think more men were injured at the 2010 Games than women? Use the data you find on the Internet and at your local library to support your answer.

For More Information

Further Reading

Bowes, Lisa. *Lucy Tries Short Track*. Victoria, BC: Orca Book Publishers, 2016.

Wallechinsky, David, and Jaime Loucky. *The Complete Book of the Winter Olympics*. Hertford, NC: Crossroad Press, 2014.

Waxman, Laura Hamilton. *Speed Skating*. Mankato, MN: Amicus Ink, 2017.

Websites

The International Olympic Committee
https://www.olympic.org/the-ioc
Discover how the IOC works to build a better world through sports.

International Skating Union
www.isu.org/en/home
Learn all about international speed skating.

Olympics—Short Track Speed Skating
https://www.olympic.org/short-track-speed-skating
Find out about the history of short track speed skating at the Olympics.

GLOSSARY

ambassadors (am-BAS-uh-derz) representatives for something, like the Olympics

chief executive officer (CHEEF ig-ZEK-yuh-tiv AW-fi-sur) the executive with the chief decision-making authority in an organization

recreational (rek-ree-AY-shuhn-al) of, relating to, or characteristic of activities like games, sports, or hobbies that you like to do in your spare time

straightaways (STRAYT-uh-wayz) sections of tracks that don't curve

tourists (TOOR-ists) people who are traveling for pleasure

venue (VEN-yoo) the place of an action or event

INDEX